DATE DUE

TIME TRAVEL GUIDES

ANCIENT CHINA

EXPRESS EDITION

Jane Shuter

Raintree

Chicago, Illinois

© 2008 Raintree
a division of Reed Elsevier Inc.
100 N. LaSalle, Suite 1200, Chicago, IL 60602

Customer Service 888–363–4266
Visit our website at www.raintreelibrary.com

Editorial: Lucy Beevor, Harriet Milles,
  and Sarah Shannon
Adaptation for Freestyle Express: Geoff Barker
  and Harriet McGregor
Design: Steve Mead, Geoff Ward, and Ian Winton
Picture Research: Ruth Blair
Illustrations: Eikon Illustration and Tim Slade
Production: Duncan Gilbert
Originated by Modern Age
Printed and bound in the United States by
Lake Book Manufacturing, Inc.

12 11 10 09 08
10 9 8 7 6 5 4 3 2 1

Library of Congress Cataloging-in-Publication Data
Shuter, Jane.
  Ancient China /Jane Shuter.
    p. cm. – (Time travel guides)
  Includes bibliographical references and index.
  ISBN-13: 978-1-4109-3038-5 (lib. bdg.)
  ISBN-10: 1-4109-3038-6 (lib. bdg.)
  ISBN-13: 978-1-4109-3045-3 (pbk.)
  ISBN-10: 1-4109-3045-9 (pbk.)
  1. China–Description and travel. I. Title.
  DS707.S56 2008
  931–dc22

                              2006033868

This leveled text is a version of Freestyle:
Time Travel Guides: Ancient China.

Acknowledgments
The publishers would like to thank the following for
permission to reproduce photographs:
AKG Images p. 36 (Erich Lessing); Alamy pp. 56–57
(imagebroker); Ancient Art & Architecture Collection Ltd.
p. 18 (B. Crisp); Art Archive pp. 54 (Berry Hill Galleries,
NY), 15, 31 (Bibliothèque Nationale, Paris), 24 (Dagli
Orti), 27 top and bottom, 40 (Musée Cernuschi, Paris/
Dagli Orti), 17, 28–29, 30 (National Palace Museum,
Taiwan), 13; Bridgeman Art Library pp. 8 (Arthur M.
Sackler Museum, Harvard University Art Museums, USA,
bequest of Grenville L. Winthrop), 19 (Bibliotheque
Nationale, Paris), 50–51, 44–45 (British Library, London),
48 (Musee Conde, Chantilly, France, Giraudon), 46
(Percival David Foundation, London), 25 (Private
Collection), 20–21 (Private Collection, © Christie's
Images); Corbis pp. 43 (Archivo Iconografico), 41, 42, 47
(Asian Art & Archaeology, Inc.), 52 (Bob Krist), 34–35
(Free Agents Ltd.), 10 (John & Lisa Merrill), 38 (Keren
Su), 6–7, 11, 37 (Liu Liqun), 47 (Royal Ontario Museum,
Canada), 16 (Werner Forman), 53; Getty Images pp. 12
(Aurora), 26 (Photodisc), 23 (Stone); Mary Evans Picture
Library p. 55; Science & Society Picture Library/Science
Museum p. 49.

Cover photograph of ancient Chinese coins reproduced
with permission of Ancient Art & Architecture Collection
Ltd./R. Kawka. Cover photograph of Mutianyu on the
Great Wall near Beijing reproduced with permission of
Corbis/Peter Guttman. Photograph of a bronze figure
head reproduced with permission of Corbis/Asian Art &
Archaeology, Inc.

The publishers would like to thank Gwen Bennett for her
assistance in the preparation of this book.

Every effort has been made to contact copyright holders
of any material reproduced in this book. Any omissions
will be rectified in subsequent printings if notice is given
to the publishers.

CONTENTS

Words that appear in the text in bold, **like this**, are explained in the glossary.

N
W E
S

SILK ROAD

THE GREAT WALL

Dunhuang

CHANG JIANG
(YANGTZE RIVER)

Chang Jiang (Yangtze River)

Huang He (Yellow River)

Chang'an

Xi Jiang (Pearl River)

Russia

Mongolia

China

India

S.E. Asia

Pacific
Ocean

MAP OF ANCIENT CHINA

Beijing

Tianjin

Hangzhou

THE GRAND CANAL

SOUTH CHINA SEA

Ancient Chinese borders

Xia Dynasty

Shang Dynasty

Qin Dynasty

Modern Chinese Border

These peaks are made of limestone. They are found in south-central China.

CHAPTER 1

FACTS ABOUT ANCIENT CHINA

The period called "Ancient China" started around 2205 BCE. That was more than 4,000 years ago. This period lasted more than 3,000 years! Ancient China is ruled by one person. When that person dies, his power passes to another family member. When one family rules for some time, this is called a **dynasty**.

Sometimes the rulers cannot keep control. These are dangerous times. Be careful when you choose to visit Ancient China!

WHEN TO GO

The best time to visit ancient China is during the Tang Dynasty (CE 618–907). That is more than 1,000 years ago. This period is called the **Golden Age** of ancient China. It is very rich and successful. You will see lots of great Tang inventions. Inventions are new things that people have created.

Another good time to visit is during the Song Dynasty. Try to arrive around CE 1000. That is about 1,000 years ago. The Song Dynasty is safest at this time.

This bronze container was made in the Shang Dynasty. The Shang bronze workers were very skillful.

ANCIENT CHINA—WHEN TO VISIT

(Note: dates given are approximate. BCE means the years before our modern calendar started. CE is the time of our modern calendars.)

Dynasty	What happened during this time?
Xia (about 2200 – about 1700 BCE)	City of Erlitou is built (this is not certain).
Shang (about 1700 – about 1050 BCE)	Silk manufacture (making) begins. China is very small at this time.
Zhou (1050–475 BCE)	First metal coins are used.
Warring States (475–221 BCE)	Different states fighting.
Qin (221–207 BCE)	First emperor brings peace. He also brings harsh punishments. Visitors are not welcome.
Han (206 BCE–CE 220)	Paper is invented. Painted silk **scrolls** (rolled paper or fabric) are used for writing. Tools are made from iron.
Three Kingdoms (CE 220–280)	Safe during the early years of this period, but only in the capital cities.
Period of disunity (CE 265–589)	Almost constant war.
Sui (CE 581–618)	Ancient China is peaceful. Grand Canal and other canals built. Lands farthest from the capital are still not safe.
Tang (CE 618–907)	There is lots of poetry and reading. There is also tea drinking and music. Emperors (rulers) are weak.
Five Dynasties (CE 907–960)	Almost constant war.
Song (CE 960–1279)	Paper money and printing is invented. The tradition of **binding** feet begins. Girls' feet are wrapped to make the feet smaller. It is believed this makes feet beautiful.

Key:

Stay away—danger!
Okay time to visit
Best time to visit—go for it!

LUNAR FESTIVALS

Try to visit ancient China when there is a festival. The Chinese calendar works on **lunar months** (see page 61). Lunar months follow the changes of the Moon.

The Chinese New Year is also called the Spring Festival. It begins on day one of the first month in the lunar calendar. It is the most important ancient Chinese festival.

Here are some more festivals:

- *Qing ming* happens on day four of the fourth moon. It celebrates the start of spring. People clean family tombs on this day. A tomb is a place where a dead person is buried.
- *Duanwu* happens on day five of the fifth moon. People race boats that look like dragons.

⚡ At Chinese New Year, people do exciting dragon dances.

BUSY CITY OR PEACEFUL COUNTRYSIDE?

If you love to shop, visit the city of Chang'an. Go during the Tang Dynasty. Chang'an is a huge city. It has two big markets. The markets sell everything from songbirds to silk shoes.

If you love the countryside, you should visit the Huang He (Yellow River). The land by the river is farmed. The farmers here grow rice and wheat. They grow beans and vegetables.

If you prefer mountains, take a boat trip along the Chang Jiang (Yangtze River).

The mountains along the Chang Jiang River are very steep.

GEOGRAPHY AND CLIMATE

Ancient China has deserts and mountains. The weather differs from place to place. The ancient Chinese wear the right clothes for the weather in their area. You should dress like the locals.

Summer **monsoons** (heavy rain) happen in the south. At this time it is very hot. There will be flooding. Floods can destroy roads or bridges. Take an emergency kit with you. Pack a tent and a blanket. Pack some dried food and a bottle of water.

The weather in these mountains is very cold.

FARMING

Most people in ancient China are farmers. They live and work on the land of rich people. They grow crops. They must give some crops to the emperor (ruler). They must also give crops to the landowners. They can keep any leftover crops.

In the north, farmers grow wheat. They also grow soybeans and vegetables. In the south farmers grow rice and red beans. They also grow tropical fruits, such as oranges. Farmers grow rice by rivers.

This modern Chinese farmer is growing rice. He is farming in a similar way to the ancient Chinese.

GOVERNMENT

Ancient China is ruled by an emperor (type of ruler). He makes all the decisions and laws (rules). The ancient Chinese emperors do not work. Other people run the country for them.

UNDERSTANDING THE SYSTEM

Shi Huangdi was the first emperor of ancient China. He divided China into 36 areas. Each area was run by three people:

- a **military leader**—to run the army
- a **governor**—to run daily life
- an inspector—to make sure the governor and military leader do what the emperor wants.

Later emperors used similar systems. They used many **officials**. Officials are people who work for the government. A government is a group of people who lead an area or country.

ANCIENT CHINESE SOCIETY

The emperor, nobles, and their families are rich. They do important jobs. Farmers are poor. The Chinese think that farmers are very important. This is because they grow food. Traders are not as important. Traders are people who sell goods, such as shoes.

BE PATIENT!

It takes a long time for the ancient Chinese officials to make decisions. Try to be patient. It is very rude to get angry.

This picture shows people taking exams. They hope to become officials.

These women are guests of a Tang emperor. They eat a feast. They sit together, not with their husbands.

FAMILY LIFE

In ancient China family life is very important. It is more important than friendship or business. The oldest man is the most important family member. Everyone has to obey him. He must look after the rest of the family.

SEPARATE LIVES

Rich families do not spend much time together. They have large homes. The women stay at home. The men spend a lot of time away from home. Poorer families mix together more. A family lives in one room.

DIFFERENT ROLES

A boy works for his family. He cares for his parents when they are old. Most will marry and have children.

Most boys do the same jobs as their fathers. Only the sons of rich families have an education.

Girls look after the home. Most girls also make cloth and sew. They must also entertain others. When a girl marries, she goes to live with her husband's family.

Here is an adult son, his wife, and their children. They are greeting his parents. Children must obey their parents all their lives.

BELIEFS

The ancient Chinese believe in gods, goddesses, and spirits. People think that they affect their lives.

The ancient Chinese believe that nature spirits come to Earth. Nature spirits are spirits of natural things, such as water or air. Nature spirits can even be ordinary people. They can bring rain and good luck. They can even bring a toothache!

This giant statue of the Buddha was carved by monks.

BUDDHISM

During the Han **Dynasty**, a new religion reached ancient China. It is called **Buddhism. Buddhists** believe you should not become too attached to material things. Material things are items you own. Buddhists also believe in treating other people well.

THE SAYINGS OF CONFUCIUS

Confucius was a famous **philosopher** in ancient China. A philosopher is a person who is wise and thinks a lot. Most ancient Chinese follow Confucius' ideas:

- Everyone should be kind to one another.
- Emperors must rule wisely.
- People must obey the emperors.
- Fathers must take care of their **households** (everyone living in the house).
- Households must obey the fathers.

DAOISM

A man called Lao Tzu taught the ideas of **Dao**. Dao means "the way." **Daoism** says that people should live in peace with each other. People should live in peace with nature. Daoism has become a religion.

This picture shows Lao Tzu riding on a water buffalo.

These men are enjoying
a meal in a garden.

CHAPTER 2

USEFUL INFORMATION

The ancient Chinese do not travel much. Most people spend their whole lives in the same place. The ancient Chinese think that travel is dangerous and difficult. You can travel by road and river. You can stay in villages and towns. Later on in the ancient Chinese period, there is more choice of places to stay.

WHAT TO WEAR

Check the weather before you travel. Take lots of thin clothes with you. You can buy silk clothes when you arrive. Silk is thin and light. It can keep you warm in cold weather. It can keep you cool in warm weather.

ANCIENT CHINESE CLOTHES

Everyone in ancient China wears robes. Robes are long, loose clothes.

- Wealthy women and men wear long robes.
- Workers wear short robes. They wear trousers underneath.
- Poor people wear clothes made of **hemp**. Hemp is a type of plant.

What you wear in ancient China shows how important you are.

Nobleman and his wife   Worker   Poor man

WOMEN'S FASHIONS

Rich women wear clothes with long, hanging sleeves. A rich woman's hair will be put up in a difficult style (see page 22). She will wear **ornaments** (decorations) in her hair.

FOOT BINDING

The ancient Chinese think that tiny feet are beautiful. In ancient China, people **bind** (tightly wrap) girls' feet. The bandages are put on when girls are about five years old. The bandages are only taken off to put on clean ones. Binding makes the feet even smaller. **Foot binding** is painful.

MONEY

The early ancient Chinese do not use money. Instead, they **barter**. When people barter, they exchange objects instead of money. People in the Shang **Dynasty** use cowrie shells to barter. These are seashells. People in the Zhou Dynasty use the first metal coins.

These round coins come from different ancient Chinese dynasties.

COINS WITH HOLES

Later on in ancient China, you will use round coins. They have a hole in the middle. You can thread them on to a string. This makes them easy to carry. You can tie the string around your waist.

Be careful in towns, though. Thieves may cut the string and run away with your money.

SWAP SHOP

Try to barter with people. Many poorer people prefer to exchange goods. You could swap a chicken for a bowl. Or perhaps trade a cabbage for some rice.

PAPER MONEY

The ancient Chinese are the first people to use paper money. They call it "flying money." This is because it is light and can blow away. The first paper money is used during the Tang Dynasty. It is just for travelers and traders.

Paper money can be used by everyone during the Song Dynasty (CE 960–1279). This is 800 to 1,000 years ago.

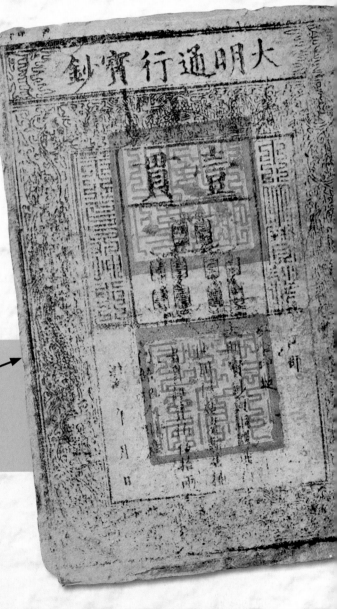

This piece of paper money is from the 13th century. This is a bit later than the period we call "ancient China."

FOOD

The food in ancient China is interesting. In the north, people eat noodles and dumplings. In the south, people eat rice.

MEALS FOR RICH AND POOR

Rich people eat lots of meat. On special occasions, they eat snakes and small birds. The rest of the time, they eat pork, chicken, or lamb. They also eat goose and duck.

Poor people eat either wheat porridge or rice. They also eat vegetables. They do not eat much meat. Poor people in the countryside grow food.

CHOPSTICKS ARE FUN!

In ancient China, you must use chopsticks to eat. Hold them as shown in the photograph. Keep the bottom chopstick steady. Move the top one to pick up the food.

EATING OUT

The ancient Chinese eat their main meal in the evening. The meal is placed in the middle of the table. People help themselves.

This bowl is used by ordinary people.

People eat cold leftover food for breakfast. During the day, there are street **vendors** (sellers) in town. They sell everything from plain noodles to rich stews.

Tea was a gift to the gods in religious ceremonies.

Litter

This ancient Chinese picture shows types of transportation. It shows horses and litters. Litters are seats attached to poles.

CHAPTER 3

GETTING AROUND

You need to know how to get around ancient China. It is a huge country. It takes a long time to get from one place to another. The journey will be uncomfortable.

In ancient China only traders travel. Traders are people who sell goods, such as silk. Most people think travel is dangerous. They think that you will meet robbers along the way.

TRAVELING BY ROAD

Ancient Chinese roads are made of soil and mud. The first emperor made a few roads. This was more than 2,000 years ago. These are the best roads. They are wider than other roads. Many roads in the countryside are narrow. In the mountains roads can be very steep.

You can walk or ride a horse along the roads. Rich people travel in a **litter**. A litter is a seat attached to poles. It is carried by servants. Servants are people who work for another person.

LIGHTING THE WAY

You can only travel by day in ancient China. There is no street lighting. This makes it hard to follow the roads at night.

TRAVELING BY BOAT

The ancient Chinese travel by water as much as possible. They use rivers and canals. They also travel by sea. In the Sui **Dynasty** you can travel on the Grand Canal. It joins two rivers together. It is more than 1,000 miles (1,600 kilometers) long.

For short journeys you can use ferries. Ferries are boats that carry people short distances. For longer journeys you could travel on a ship. You might have to sleep on deck. You may sleep in the **hold** (bottom of the ship).

An emperor traveling on the Grand Canal.

WHERE TO STAY

You can stay at different types of inns. An inn is a kind of hotel. In the cheapest inn, you share a room with other travelers. Everyone eats and sleeps in one room. There will not be any toilets or bedding.

In more expensive inns, there will be separate rooms for eating and sleeping. You will be given water to wash with. There will be toilets near the main building.

AN HONORED GUEST

You might stay at an ancient Chinese family's home. This is a great honor. Family homes are very private. You will be given the best of everything they have.

CHOOSING A GIFT

If you stay in a family home, you should take the family a gift. Be careful though! It is rude to give a cheap gift. Do not give an expensive gift either. The family will think you are showing off. The best gift is something that takes you time and effort. A poem would be a good gift.

↙ This is the home of a noble family.

Noble families live in big homes. Nobles are rich
people. Their homes are built around two courtyards.
A courtyard is an open space. The first courtyard is
for visitors. The second courtyard is for women
and children.

LIFE IN A VILLAGE

In a village, families live in one room. Most village
life happens outside in the fields. In a small village,
almost everyone comes from the same family.

This is the modern Great Wall of China. It follows the line of the ancient Great Wall.

CHAPTER 4

WHAT TO SEE AND DO

There is lots to see and do in ancient China. You can rest in the countryside. You can go to the cities to explore and shop. There are also some "must see" places. Whatever you do you must visit the Great Wall.

THE GREAT WALL

The Great Wall is amazing. It is 4,160 miles (6,700 kilometers) long. It does not follow a straight path. In some places there are three layers of wall.

The Great Wall was not built all at once. Early Chinese rulers started it. They wanted to keep out invaders from the north.

The early Great Wall was built of soil and pebbles. It was also built of reeds (plants) and wood. Over time the soil was replaced with stone.

GREAT WALL FACTS

Length: 4,160 miles (6,700 kilometers)
Workers: criminals—this included thieves and murderers
Deaths among workers: about 1 death for every 5 feet (1.5 meters) of wall
Extra workers: elephants did some of the heavy lifting.

The countryside around the Great Wall is varied. It changes from snowy mountains to flat farmland.

PEACE AND QUIET

On your trip, visit the Great Wall. Then relax in the countryside. You could go to the cold northern mountains. You could have a magical night in the desert. It will be completely dark. The only light comes from your campfire and the stars.

There are many inns in the beautiful countryside. You might want to travel along a river. River travel can be very peaceful. If there is a storm, river travel can be exciting, too!

DUNHUANG

Dunhuang is a city. It is in the west of ancient China. It is on the Silk Road. The Silk Road is a route taken by traders. Lots of traders and visitors travel to Dunhuang. They come from many different countries.

Dunhuang is also a famous meeting place. **Buddhists** and **scholars** meet here. Scholars are people who study a certain subject. Many Buddhists and scholars live in caves in the mountains in Dunhuang.

Here there are many temples to Buddha. Buddha is the god that Buddhists worship.

Temple in the caves near Dunhuang.

CHANG'AN

Chang'an is a city. It is also on the Silk Road. Chang'an is a city of emperors. During the Han **Dynasty**, over half of the city is just palaces for the emperor!

During the Tang Dynasty, Chang'an is a huge city. More than one million people live here. Palaces and government buildings are separate from the rest of the city. This is called the Imperial area. Do not go there. You could be executed (killed) if caught!

WHAT TO SEE IN CHANG'AN

This is a map of the city of Chang'an. Watch for the high **watchtowers**. Soldiers in the watchtowers look out over the city.

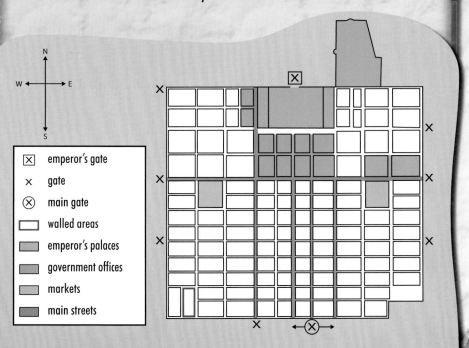

⊠	emperor's gate
×	gate
⊗	main gate
▭	walled areas
▮	emperor's palaces
▮	government offices
▮	markets
▮	main streets

ENTERTAINMENT

In ancient China entertainment happens in the street. In the market place you will find musicians and singers. You will find acrobats and dancers.

Street entertainers like the audience to join in. Sing along with the singer. You don't have to keep quiet. Most of the audience will be chatting.

CAGED BIRDS

The ancient Chinese keep caged birds. The birds' owners meet in teahouses. Being together makes the birds sing more. You can sit and drink tea. You can listen to the birds.

This bowl is decorated with acrobats. Acrobats were also popular decorations on cups.

PRIVATE SHOWS

Emperors and nobles have their own musicians and acrobats. Less wealthy (poorer) people hire street entertainers. They do this for special occasions.

Some people write poetry. They read it to family and friends. Many wealthy people make music. Girls from wealthy families learn to play musical instruments. They also learn to sing and dance.

These are bells from the tomb of a **governor** (ruler). A tomb is a place where a dead person is buried. Each bell can make two notes.

GAMES

Almost everyone in ancient China plays games. Dominoes and backgammon are popular. The ancient Chinese also invented card games. Rich women play a lot of cards.

Have a go at playing ancient Chinese dominoes! The ancient Chinese play with two sets of dominoes at a time. One set has pictures. One set has numbers. There are lots of rules. It is hard to remember them all.

The ancient Chinese often carry games like this one in their large sleeves.

Many ancient Chinese enjoy word games. They also make up poetry. These word games let rich people show off their education. Poor people don't play these games.

These nobles are playing polo. This is a game played on horseback.

SPORT

The ancient Chinese enjoy sports. People go to **cockfighting** matches. In these matches cocks (male chickens) are made to fight each other.

ANCIENT CHINESE INVENTIONS?

The ancient Chinese may have invented (created) these sports:

- Soccer. Chinese soccer has two teams. It uses a leather ball stuffed with silk.
- Golf. Golf clubs have bamboo handles.
- Badminton. Two people hit a "birdie" (feathered ball) to each other.

Stores line the main road in this ancient Chinese town. The stores are the front parts of the shopkeepers' homes.

CHAPTER 5

SHOPPING

Ancient Chinese towns are full of shops and markets. Markets are good places to buy silk and **porcelain**. Porcelain is a type of pottery. A pack of Chinese cards would make a good present. You could also buy yourself a beautiful kite.

TRADITIONAL SOUVENIRS

SILK

In ancient China silk is used to make clothes and bedding. It is also used to make rope. People write and paint on silk.

The market sells many different colors of silk. But you won't find any yellow silk. Only the emperor and his family can wear yellow.

PORCELAIN

Another great souvenir is **porcelain**. Porcelain is a type of pottery. It is very hard and smooth. Only the ancient Chinese know how to make porcelain. They trade it at a high price. If you want to buy porcelain, visit during the Song **Dynasty**.

The "cracks" in this dish are made on purpose. They give it a special look.

LACQUER

Another famous ancient Chinese product is **lacquer**. Lacquer is a shiny coating. It is made from the **sap** (juice) of the lacquer tree. It is used to make combs and bowls.

To make a lacquer bowl, the sap is colored with crushed rock. Then it is painted onto an object. It must be put on in layers. Some pieces of lacquer have up to 200 layers.

A GOOD PRESENT
This is a lacquer bowl. Lacquer is beautiful and very shiny. It is not damaged by heat or water.

JADE

Jade is a precious stone. The ancient Chinese use it to make jewelry and **ornaments** (decorations). It is difficult to carve. Even a simple bracelet can take days to make.

This brooch is made of jade. It is in the shape of a dragon.

AMAZING GIFTS

The ancient Chinese are very good at inventing (creating) things. Their creations can be very interesting.

PAPER

Why not take some paper home? Paper was invented in Han times. You can copy ancient Chinese writing. Buy some paper and brushes. You will also need ink. Ink is sold as a heavy, solid block. You have to scrape ink off the block. Then you mix it with water.

Paper lanterns or kites also make good gifts. Take home a pack of ancient Chinese cards. You can teach your friends to play.

FLY YOUR KITE

The ancient Chinese make beautiful kites. Some kites are shaped like dragons and butterflies.

WATER CLOCKS AND FIREWORKS

A water clock is an unusual present. Water flows from a tank into 36 buckets. The buckets are on a wheel. The buckets collect water as they move. This moves the workings of the clock.

This is an ancient Chinese compass. A compass helps you find your way. The needle of this compass always points south.

You could take home some fireworks. The ancient Chinese invented gunpowder. Gunpowder is black powder that explodes. It is used to make fireworks. You can even buy fireworks on tiny skis. They shoot across water.

A Chinese patient
visiting her doctor.

CHAPTER 6

KEEPING SAFE AND WELL

Try to keep safe and well on your trip to ancient China. You don't want to be the victim of a crime. You may need a doctor, though. Luckily medicine in ancient China is very good. The crime rate is low. Just don't commit a crime. The punishments are horrible!

Today, Chinese medicine uses similar treatments as in ancient China.

STAYING HEALTHY

To stay healthy in ancient China, only drink clean water. You can drink from rivers in the countryside. Do not drink water from rivers in towns. People throw garbage into the river. Sometimes they even use the river as a toilet.

If you need a doctor, go to a big town. There will be several doctors. Doctors usually work at home. If there is no town, the village people may help you.

HOW TO PAY

Many ancient Chinese pay their doctors to keep them well. They visit them a lot. A sick person will not pay a doctor. This is because the doctor has not kept the person healthy.

ANCIENT CHINESE MEDICINE

Ancient Chinese medicine is based on the flow of **energy** around the body. Energy is the power to do work. They call this energy *qi* (say "chee"). The ancient Chinese say that your energy should flow smoothly. If your energy flow is blocked, you will feel unwell. Food and exercise can affect your *qi*.

HERBAL CURES

The ancient Chinese use herbs to cure people. These cures are still used today. The ancient Chinese use willow bark to reduce pain. Modern aspirin is similar to willow bark.

ACUPUNCTURE

Acupuncture involves inserting needles into the body. They must go in at exact "points." This gets the *qi* flowing.

This diagram shows some of the 360 acupuncture points.

STAYING SAFE

Keep your money in a safe place. Do not hang your money string on your belt.

Report any crime to the **magistrate**. The magistrate is a person who decides if a crime has happened. Policemen and **officials** help the magistrate decide. Officials are government workers.

The magistrate is sitting at the table. The criminal kneels in chains.

POLITE LAWS

From the start of the Qin **Dynasty**, laws change. They are not just about crime. People have to be polite, too. For example, it is the law to respect your parents.

A RANGE OF PUNISHMENTS

The best punishment is a beating. The worst punishment is to have your head chopped off. Some criminals have to wear a wide wooden collar. This is called a *cangue*.

This photo was taken in the 1890s. It shows a collar called a cangue. These women are being punished.

Chinese writing has a series of symbols like these. The symbols are called "characters."

CHAPTER 7

ANCIENT CHINA: FACTS AND FIGURES

This section will help you on your trip to ancient China. You can look up **dynasties** and inventions. You can also check out the dates of the major festivals. There are lists of books that will help you to learn more about ancient China.

ANCIENT CHINA PHRASE BOOK

WRITTEN ANCIENT CHINESE

The ancient Chinese writing uses symbols not letters. The symbols are called characters. The characters can join together to make a new word. Chinese characters change over time. It depends on when you visit (see below).

SPOKEN ANCIENT CHINESE

There are many spoken languages in ancient China. How you say a word can change its meaning. So the same word can have many meanings.

	Shang	Zhou	Warring States	Qin onward
rén (nin) human				
nu(nra?) woman				
er (nha?) ear				
ma (mra?) horse				
yú (nha) fish				
shan (sran) mountain				
rì (nit) sun				
yuè (not) moon				
yu (wha?) rain				
yun (wan) cloud				

WRITTEN NUMBERS

In ancient China written numbers change over time.
These are from the Shang Dynasty (see page 9).

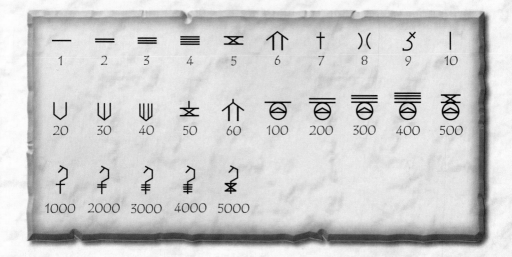

Officials (government workers) use counting boards.
These boards are rows of nine squares. Rods of
bamboo are put in the boards to show numbers.
People write numbers in a similar way (see below).

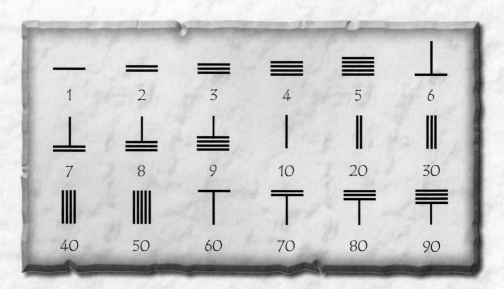

ANCIENT CHINA AT A GLANCE

(BCE means the years before our modern calendar started. CE is the time of our modern calendar.)

TIMELINE

Xia (about 2200–about 1700 BCE) 4,200–3,700 years ago — City of Erlitou may have been built.

Shang (about 1700–about 1050 BCE) 3,700–3,000 years ago — Bronze working is very advanced. The first writing that we can read.

Zhou (1050–475 BCE) 3,000–2,500 years ago — Confucius is teaching.

Warring States (475–221 BCE) (2,500–2,200 years ago) — The Zhou Kingdom is broken up into different kingdoms. A kingdom is an area ruled by a king. They fight.

Qin Dynasty (221–207 BCE) 2,200 years ago — First Emperor introduces money and weights. He introduces measures and writing. The Great Wall is built.

Han Dynasty (206 BCE–CE 220) 2,200-1,800 years ago — **Buddhism** reaches China. Paper is invented.

Three Kingdoms (CE 220–280) 1,800 years ago — China is divided into three kingdoms. First book printed.

Period of disunity (CE 265–589) 1,750–1,400 years ago — The three kingdoms divide into more kingdoms.

Sui Dynasty (CE 581–618) 1,400 years ago — Buddhism becomes more popular. Grand Canal is built. **Porcelain** is invented. Porcelain is a type of pottery.

Tang Dynasty (CE 618–907) 1,400–1,100 years ago — Tea is drunk widely. Gunpowder is invented.

Five Dynasties (CE 907–960) 1,100–1,040 years ago — Gunpowder is used in war.

Song Dynasty (CE 960–1279) 1,040–700 years ago — Paper money and printing are introduced.

CE 1279 About 700 years ago — Mongols take over ancient China. They create their own dynasty, the Yuan.

THE LUNAR CALENDAR

The lunar calendar follows the changes of the Moon. The months have no names. They are just called first moon, second moon, and so on.

- 12 months = 1 year
- 30 days = 1 month
- 1 week = 10 days

DATES OF FESTIVALS

The Chinese New Year (Spring Festival) begins on the first day of the first moon.

Qing Ming begins on the fourth day of the fourth moon.

Duanwu begins on the fifth day of the fifth moon.

Chong Yang begins on the seventh day of the seventh moon.

Zhong Qiu fifteenth day of the eighth moon.

Dong Zhi at the winter solstice in the eleventh moon. The winter solstice is the shortest day of the year. This day has the least amount of sunshine.

Laba the eighth day of the twelfth moon.

FURTHER READING

BOOKS

Challen, Paul C. *Peoples of the Ancient World: Life in Ancient China.*
New York: Crabtree Publishing Company, 2004.

Cotterell, Arthur and Buller, Laura. *Eyewitness Guide: Ancient China.*
New York: DK, 2005.

Schomp, Virginia. *People of the Ancient World: The Ancient Chinese.*
Danbury: Franklin Watts, 2005.

WEBSITES

- http://www.historyforkids.org/learn/china/index.htm
- http://members.aol.com/Donnclass/Chinalife.html
- http://www.tourroundchina.com/festival.htm

GLOSSARY

barter to exchange things of a similar value, rather than using money

bind wrap up very tightly

Buddhism religion based on the teachings of Buddha (name given to Siddhartha Gautama)

Buddhists people who follow the teachings of Buddha. They believe you should not become too attached to material things (things you own).

cockfighting making male chickens (cocks) fight each other

Dao the idea that people should live in peace with nature and with each other

Daoism religion developed in ancient China that follows the ideas of Dao

dynasty period of time when a single family rules a country

energy power to do work

foot binding tightly tying girls' feet to make them smaller

Golden Age period of time when a country is at its wealthiest, is well ruled, and makes new discoveries

governor person who runs part of a country for the ruler of the country

hemp plant that is used to make rope or cloth

hold (of a ship) place at the bottom of a ship where things are stored

household everyone living in the same house

jade hard precious stone

lacquer shiny coating made from the sap of the lacquer tree

litter large seat with curtain all around that is carried by poles underneath

lunar month month that follows the 30-day movement of the Moon

magistrate someone who decides if a person has broken the law, and punishes that person if he thinks they have

military leader person in charge of an army

monsoon season of heavy rains

official person working for the government

ornament object used for decoration

philosopher someone who studies the purpose of life

polo sport where a ball is hit into a goal by men riding horses. The men hit the ball with long sticks.

porcelain type of pottery made with a clay called kaolin that can be baked at a high temperature until very hard and smooth

sap juice inside a plant or tree

scholar someone who studies a particular subject

scroll long, thin roll of paper or fabric

vendor someone who sells something

watchtower high, protected place where soldiers can keep watch

INDEX